LORD BERESFORD AND LADY FLO

Lord Delaval James Beresford in 1906, a few months before he was killed in December.

Florida J. Wolfe, "Lady Flo," 1906.

The train wreck on the Minneapolis, St. Paul and Sault St. Marie Railroad in which Lord Delaval was killed. Note the telescoped coach.

SOUTHWESTERN STUDIES

MONOGRAPH No. 25

Lord Beresford
and
Lady Flo

by

Eugene O. Porter

$5 CLOTH

ABOUT THE AUTHOR

EUGENE O. PORTER retired in 1969 as Emeritus Professor of History at The University of Texas at El Paso. He received the A. B. degree in history from Ohio Wesleyan University, and the M. A. and Ph. D. from Ohio State University. Porter taught at The University of Texas at El Paso from 1940, except for three years during World War II and two years during the Korean conflict when he was serving in the armed forces. Recognized as an authority on Marxism and Communism, he has lectured extensively in the Southwest, and his book *Fallacies of Karl Marx* was published by the Texas Western Press in 1962. Porter has produced several scholarly monographs and articles about his field of study. He has served as editor of *Password*, quarterly magazine of the El Paso County Historical Society, since its founding in 1956, and his interest in Lord Beresford and Lady Flo is a result of his editorship of this publication and his interest in unusual historical events in the Southwest.

LORD BERESFORD AND LADY FLO

by Eugene O. Porter

El Pasoans first read of the death of Lord Delaval[1] James Beresford at the breakfast table on Monday, December 24, 1906. In a one-and-one-half-column item on page one, over a St. Paul, Minnesota, dateline of December 23rd, the *El Paso Morning Times* screamed: *Nine Killed in a Railway Wreck — Among the Dead is Lord D. J. Beresford of Casas Grandes.*

Reports on Lord Delaval's Death

An interesting fact concerning the various newspaper accounts of the wreck is that all emphasized the importance of the Beresford family rather than the deceased. The *Sheldon Progress* of Enderlin, North Dakota,[2] for instance, under the heading:

"A Distinguished Family," explained that, Lord Delaval Beresford belonged to the well known Irish family of that name. He was presumably a son of the late Marquis of Waterford and a brother of the present Marquis and Lords Charles, Marcus and William Beresford. A cablegram was received in Minneapolis yesterday from Lord Waterford at the family seat in the south of Ireland requesting that the body be held for instructions. Lord Charles Beresford is the famous British admiral; Lord William served with distinction in the army and won the Victoria Cross for an act of heroism in the Zulu war. Lord Marcus devotes his attentions to the turf. He was for years official starter to the Jockey Club and later took charge of King Edward's racing stud. The dead man had lived in America many years and had large cattle ranches in Texas[3] and at Medicine Hat.

The *El Paso Herald* likewise emphasized the family's importance. The headline on the front page: *Lord Admiral's Brother Killed in Wreck,* was in type so large and bold that it smothered the short and partly inaccurate story that followed:[4]

He [Lord Delaval] was a full brother of the lord admiral of the British Navy, and might some day have succeeded to the title of lord, as the lord admiral is said to have no children. Delaval Beresford was the next oldest brother and in line for the title should he have outlived the lord admiral.

[3]

All of this interest in the Beresford family would seem strange, if it were true, as some later insisted that Lord Delaval had lost all contact with his home and that, in fact, he had been disowned because of his excessive drinking and his coterie of companions. It was claimed, for instance, that Admiral Lord Charles visited Mexico and that "he did not even reply to Delaval's invitation to visit him."[5] Actually, Lord Charles made a hurried business trip to Mexico City in 1903. At that time, Lord Delaval was in England, and he saw his brother when the latter returned home. In refutation, it should be noted that Lord Delaval visited Ireland several times after coming to America, and also that he corresponded regularly with his brothers, although he heard more frequently from Marcus, for Charles was often absent from home on sea duty.[6] There is no evidence, indeed, that a lack of rapport existed between Lord Delaval and his family. As a matter of fact, one relative, an unidentified cousin, visited Lord Delaval sometime in the 'nineties and, it may be interesting to add, lost $1,200.00 within a few minutes at roulette in El Paso's Wigwam saloon.[7]

However that may be, it should be noted that one newspaper, the *El Paso Morning Times,* mentioned one of the Lord's companions, a Negro woman. So far as research can determine, this was the second time the two were associated in print. The first was in the *El Paso City Directory, 1898-99.* Listed in the B's was "Beresford, Delaval J., Ojitos, Chihuahua, Mex." and in the W's, "Wolfe, Flora (c.), housekpr. Delaval J. Beresford, r. same." No El Paso address was given but several older El Pasoans remember them as living on the corner of Third and South Ochoa streets (417 South Ochoa), a property Miss Wolfe purchased after Lord Delaval's death and where she lived until her death in 1913.

The *Times* story noted above, purportedly told how the two met:[8]

Some fifteen years ago, while in the city of New Orleans, [Lord Delaval] was stricken with yellow fever. A Negro woman, out of sympathy for him, nursed him and brought him through safely. When he recovered he was so grateful to the Negro woman that he took her to Mexico with him and she has lived at his ranch ever since and been a companion to him. She always came to El Paso with him, had appeared here only a few days ago, presumably for the purpose of meeting him upon his return from Canada.

A Fatal Train Wreck

Returning now to the train wreck itself, the tragedy occurred at 2:15 a.m. on Sunday on the Minneapolis, St. Paul and Sault St. Marie Railroad, popularly known as the Soo line.[9] Passenger train No. 106, eastbound, was about two and one-half hours late and running at high speed through the "stormy, foggy night" in an attempt to make up lost

time. Rounding a curve just before entering the yards at Enderlin,
North Dakota, it plowed into the rear of a switch engine occupying its
right-of-way. The two engines became one; the steel-framed baggage
car completely telescoped the wooden smoker (see photograph)[10] and
"the human beings in the latter were caught like rats in a trap."[11]

A more detailed account of the wreck was published in the *Valley
City* (North Dakota) *Times-Record*. The article related to the construc-
tion of the cars comprising the passenger train. It stated that "the train
was made up in a manner which invites manslaughter." Continuing,
the item noted that "the smoker in which the slaughter occurred was
preceded by a modern, steel-framed and heavy baggage coach. Next
came an old-fashioned, non-vestibuled, light wooden-framed smoking
car. This was followed by a modern, vestibuled, heavy steel-framed
passenger coach. The engine struck an obstruction, the weakest link
in the chain gave way and the smoker was telescoped by the baggage
coach." Eight persons were killed at the time of the impact and thirty-
five injured, three of whom died within a couple of days.[12] Interestingly
enough, the *Sheldon Progress* of Enderlin, North Dakota, listed Lord
Delaval as being from El Paso, Texas.

With the death of Lord Delaval James Beresford and the revelation
in print that he had a Negro housekeeper, a bag of tales, based almost
entirely upon hearsay, developed about the couple. Oddly enough, not
one of the three articles which have been published about this interesting and unusual pair was the result of research. Two, written by Alfred
O. Boyd and Eve Ball, and Bill McGaw,[13] were based wholly on hearsay — "as I remember them," so to speak — and the third, penned by
Colin Rickards, was purlioned from the two.[14] Further, not one of the
three mentioned the housekeeper's true name; she was called only Lady
Flo, and thus as Lady Flo is she recorded in the tales of the Southwest.

The "Northern Death Account"

One of the first of the "tales" on Lord Delaval concerned his where-
abouts in the North and his reason for being there at the time of his
death. All of the contemporary newspapers noted that he was returning
to El Paso from his ranch in Canada. The *El Paso Morning Times*
stated: "About two months ago he [Lord Delaval] passed through El
Paso, en route to Canada, where he also owned a large cattle ranch.
Before leaving El Paso he left his Canadian address with Charles
Christley,[15] the hackman. This address was Medicine Hat,[16] Alberta,[17]
Canada, which is the address given in the Associated Press report of
the accident."[18]

As if to give further emphasis to the fact that Lord Delaval was in

Canada just previous to his death, the *Times* carried a story to the effect that about three weeks before the wreck a report arrived in El Paso that he had committed suicide in Medicine Hat. According to the *Times,* Christley "sent a telegram to that place to ascertain if there was any truth in the report." Lord Delaval replied that he was "alive and well and that the report was absolutely without foundation."[19]

Yet the fact that Lord Delaval had a ranch in Canada was soon forgotten or conveniently ignored. None of the three writers mentioned above says anything about a Canadian ranch. Instead, as time passed, a tale took root that Lord Delaval had gone North to make contracts with ranchers for fattening his beeves. It is true that many ranchers in the Southwest at that time transported their cattle to Montana, the Dakotas or Minnesota to fatten on the good grass in those states[20] and it was logical to believe that Lord Delaval may have followed this practice. It could be, therefore, that logic replaced truth and the fact that Lord Delaval had a ranch in Canada was ignored.

Some Conflicting Stories

The reason this "northern states' tale" is herein labored is that it does not agree with other tales concerning Lord Delaval. One in particular claimed that the Lord was "off his rocker," that he "was going slowly out of his mind."[21] Would Lady Flo, who is credited by the lord's detractors with being the "brains of the outfit," have permitted him to go north to make contracts if he were *non compos mentis?* Too, if his feeble-mindedness were as evident as is claimed, would the northern ranchers have been willing to make contracts with him? The tale is absurd, but not so ridiculous as the one that he was *not killed* in the wreck. According to this story:

A lot of people say that Lord Beresford died in a train wreck, but he didn't. That was just a story they tell to cover up the true facts. The truth of the matter is Lord Beresford sort of went off his rocker, from drinking, I guess, and his brother Charles, came over here and got him and I guess took him back to England and put him in a institution. Anyway, they took him away from here a very sick man.[22]

A similar version is repeated by Rickards: "To avoid the scandal of admitting his madness a story was put out that Lord Delaval Beresford had been killed in a train crash while on his way to Montana to select rangeland. It is still widely believed in New Mexico."[23]

As for the "off his rocker" tale, the truth is that it was an El Pasoan who identified Lord Delaval as a victim of the train wreck and who also notified his family in England of his death. When the lord's body was taken out of the wreck and examined for documents by which to identify it, among the papers were found letters to Beresford from Judge Leigh Clark of El Paso. The authorities in Enderlin telegraphed Judge Clark that a man supposed to be D. J. Beresford, and having letters on his person from the judge, was killed in the wreck. Judge Clark immediately contacted the Enderlin authorities and also sent a cable to Lord Delaval's brothers, informing them of their brother's death.[24] Mr. Ed Anthony of El Paso, an intimate friend of Lord Delaval, then hurried to Minneapolis to identify the body.[25]

Other tales concerning Lord Delaval's death accept the fact that he was killed in a train wreck but offer different versions. One version is to the effect that he had accompanied some cattle on a train to Montana where he was killed in a train wreck.[26] A columnist for the *Calgary* (Alberta) *Herald* stated that "Beresford was killed in a train wreck at Medicine Hat."[27] In another column the same writer noted that Beresford "would not have been killed if he had been in the coach in front of the caboose, rather than in one of the stock cars entertaining some tramps."[28] Another Canadian writer quotes Hansel Gordon (Happy Jack) Jackson, foreman of Lord Delaval's Canadian ranch, that he would not have been killed "if he had minded his own business and stayed in the coach which was on the end next to the caboose. The way it was, Jack [sic] Beresford was up in the middle of the train in an empty car with a couple of bottles of whiskey entertaining some tramps on their way to Chicago."[29] Still another writer stated: "He was sitting in the smoking car when the train lurched off the track, upsetting cars and flying possessions and baggage across the right-of-way. Passengers in most of the coaches escaped and only a few of those in the smoking car were injured but Beresford was killed."[30] Evidently, Lord Delaval at long last was punished for his drinking.

Other Confused Accounts

Be that as it may, a more serious error among the "tales" robs Lord Delaval James Beresford of his individuality and also of his parentage. For some unknown reason, Canadian writers insisted upon calling him "Lord John" and "Lord Jack." Ken Liddell in the *Calgary Herald* called him "John George De Laval Beresford" and added: "It is doubtful if he was a lord in the British peerage. The Beresford family is well represented but John George De Laval Beresford is not mentioned."[31] Another writer referred to "Lord Jack" as "Viscount John Beresford, a wealthy Englishman operating in New Mexico." This same writer changed Lady Flo's name to "Lady Lou."[32] (Shades of Robert W. Service!). An El Paso newspaperman called Lord Delaval "Lord Brelsford."[33] One tale has him confused with his brother, Charles: "Lord

Beresford was once Lord Admiral of the British Navy and the way I heard it he was horribly disappointed in love. He resigned everything in England and left for Cuba, where he had a friend named Edmund De Goncer."[34]

Perhaps the most ridiculous tale was told by Dee Harkey, who served as a peace officer in New Mexico from 1893 to 1911. Harkey, who went down into Mexico in search of a fugitive, not only changed the spelling of Lord Delaval's family name but also changed his pigmentation. As Harkey told it:

> The first night out, we stayed near a Mormon colony, and they were the only people we saw enroute except a ranchman whom my pilot [guide] called 'Lord Bearsford.' He talked so much about this ranch and Lord Bearsford that I got interested in seeing them. The third night, we rode up to a ranch house which was by a little river, and the pilot said that this was Lord Bearsford's house. I went in to meet the gentleman. I knocked on the door and a big, old, black negro woman came to the door. I asked if Lord Bearsford was at home and she said 'yes, he is down about two miles from here building a fence.' When we got near the outfit, I saw a big Black Negro and a bunch of Mexicans. I asked the pilot, 'where do you suppose Lord Bearsford is?' The pilot pointed to the Negro and said, 'That's Lord Bearsford.' I replied, 'The devil it is.'
>
> 'Well, sir,' the pilot declared. 'He is a very rich man. He owns ten thousand cattle and lots of sheep and a big ranch.'[35]

It would be foolish to pursue this story in search for the truth. The most that can be said is that Harkey's description of the Negro woman as "big, old, black" did not fit Lady Flo. She was not "big" in the sense of "thickness" or "broadness." She is described by all who knew her as tall, five feet eight or nine inches, slender and very graceful, that "she walked with the grace of elegance — people looked up to her."[36] Nor was she old, Even at the time of death she was a comparatively young woman. But as for her color or, more precisely, shade of color, there is a well of confusion. At the time of Lord Delaval's death, one newspaper referred to her as the "mulatto Negress"[37] and another as the "octaroon housekeeper."[38] She was also described as "ebony-black."[39] On the other hand, Mrs. Helen G. Gameros (see footnote 36) insists that Lady Flo was brown and "could have been mistaken for a Mexican." The photograph of Lady Flo tends to confirm the description given by Mrs. Gameros.

A number of tales are current among the Anglo-American ranchers in present-day Mexico concerning Lord Delaval. Mrs. Curtis Morris,[40] now living in El Paso, repeated some of them "for what they are worth." She spent thirty-odd years ranching with her husband in northern Mexico. She did not know Lord Delaval as she was a small child when he was killed. One tale is to the effect that Lord Delaval was greatly disappointed in love. With a feeling of extreme defeatism he gave up everything and drifted to America as a remittance man, defined as a person living abroad on remittances from home. Another tale has him married but, for some unknown reason, his wife refused to join him in America. To show his love and possibly to entice her to cross the sea, he reputedly built on his Canadian ranch an exact replica of Curraghmore (see photograph), his boyhood home in Ireland.

This tale of unrequited love, which is continually cropping up in stories about Lord Delaval, may be true, but it is not true that he had a wife in England. Burke's *Peerage,* the "Bible" of the British nobility, lists Lord Delaval as "dying unmarried." And Geoffrey Bennett, in his biography of Admiral Lord Charles Beresford, writes of Lord Delaval's "subsequent death, unmarried, in a railway accident in 1906."[41] For the nonce, whether or not he was married to Lady Flo may be ignored. As for the Canadian ranch house, it contained only three rooms. One was the "bull room" where the hired hands slept; another was a combination living quarters and kitchen used by the ranch foreman; and the third was the "blue parlor" which Lord Delaval and Lady Flo occupied during their visits to the ranch.[42] As an aside, the beautiful mahogany and walnut bed of the "blue parlor" is now in the Medicine Hat Historical Museum (see photograph).[43]

Lady Flo Meets Lord Delaval

Other tales concerning Lord Delaval and Lady Flo have to do with where and how they met. One has the couple meeting in Haiti. According to this version, Lord Delaval and his English friend, Edmund De Goncer, went from Cuba to Haiti. Shortly after their arrival De Goncer returned to Cuba to sell his plantations. He intended to return to Haiti and the two planned to go to Mexico to investigate ranching possibilities. Meanwhile, Lord Delaval came down with yellow fever. He was "close to death" when a native girl named Flo nursed him back to health. Later, after he was settled on his ranch in Mexico, he sent for her.[44] A second tale differs largely as to geography; this version states that Flo was from the "Deep South" and that Lord Delaval came down with either yellow fever or malaria "in either New Orleans or Mobile."[45]

A third tale has the couple meeting in El Paso. As the story goes, Flo was brought to El Paso by a Negro army officer. After a while he deserted her and she was forced to accept employment as a barmaid. One night Lord Delaval's two drinking companions showed up at her saloon without him. Flo was told that he was in his hotel room on the verge of death from pneumonia. She took off her apron and went to his bedside where she remained until he had completely recovered.

A variation of this story has Flo, after the officer abandoned her, working for three years as a housekeeper for a wealthy rancher from whom she learned the cattle business. When the rancher sold his property, Flo came to El Paso and became a barmaid. It was then that she met Lord Delaval and nursed him to health. This version gives logic to the claim of Alfred O. Boyd, whose father was a neighbor rancher and at one time Lord Delaval's foreman, that Lady Flo took over the Beresford ranch and managed it "much better than [it] had been previously." Boyd, who evidently disliked Lord Delaval, pictured him as a "remittance man and a drunkard" who "knew nothing of ranching." On the other hand, Boyd had nothing but praise for Lady Flo. He also claimed that she was well educated, that she had attended school in Ohio and for a time had been "a fellow student of William Jennings Bryan."[46] It is true that Lady Flo and Bryan were both from Salem, Illinois, but he was several years her senior.

These "nursing tales," so to speak, seem rather strange since Lady Flo herself denied in print that she had ever nursed Lord Delaval through an illness. In fact, she said that she had never been in New Orleans. She had gone from her home in Illinois to Kansas and thence to Mexico with a relative of the former governor of Kansas, George Anthony. She and Lord Beresford had "met in the city of Chihuahua and formed a mutual liking for one another." At the time she was a nurse in the home of the American Consul in that city. Lord Delaval "induced her," she said, "to give up her position and go and live with him."[47] This she did.

Lady Flo As A Rancher

Other tales abound about Lady Flo. One pertains to her ability as a rancher. According to Boyd, Admiral Lord Charles approached his father with the complaint:

"This Negress seems to feel that she is entitled to a share of my brother's property."

Father replied: "When she took over Los Ojitos your brother was close to bankruptcy. He was drinking so much that he was incapable of handling the ranch.

Flo put it on a business basis. She paid the debts, helped him accumulate land and guided his investments. In consequence, the property, not including cattle, is worth $250,000.00.

Half or more of them in her brand. Those nobody can touch. The rest are worth, at market price, easily $50,000.00."

"But she wants a share of the land! How much can she get?"

"Not being an attorney, I couldn't say. But if you can get her to settle out of court for $100,000.00 you are fortunate."

Boyd adds that "Sir Charles Beresford took father's advice."[48]

Rickards gives another version as to the source of $100,000.00 Lady Flo is supposed to have realized from Lord Delaval's estate. According to him, she sold Los Ojitos ranch for $100,000.00 to E. K. Warren, a corset manufacturer from Michigan.[49] That Warren was a corset maker and from Michigan is not important, but relevance does come from the fact that makers of tales seem to believe that details give their stories a ring of authenticity.

This large sum of money fits in with a tale told to Bill McGaw by a little old man named Lorenzo McClellan who took up residence in the Columbus, New Mexico, jail when McGaw was living in Columbus. McClellan claimed that Lady Flo built a rooming house, "a magnificent structure," on 16th of September Street in Juárez. She is supposed to have died there, according to McClellan.[50] Actually, Lady Flo died in El Paso and the only property owned by her in Mexico at the time of death, according to her will, consisted of two city lots, valued at seventy-five dollars each, in Nuevas Casas Grandes.

The Beresford Family

The Beresford family[51] is an ancient and honorable one within the hierarchy of the British nobility.[52] Its lineage on the distaff side goes back to a Breton family from Poher, sometime Poer, that went to England with William the Conqueror and later moved to Ireland in the "wake of Strongbow." Adrian IV, the only Englishman ever to be Pope, gave Ireland as a fief to King Henry II in 1154. Twelve years later the King of Leinster, pressed by rivals, appealed to Henry for help. The English King allowed Richard de Clare, Earl of Pembroke, known as "Strongbow," to recruit an expedition to aid Leinster. But Henry became apprehensive of the increasing power of the Earl and decided to visit Ireland in person. He was able to secure the submission of most of the native rulers and before returning to England in 1172 left a number of officials to represent him. One of these was Robert (sometimes given as Roger) De La Poer, Henry's Knight Marshal. He was appointed Joint Governor of Ireland with Hugh de Lacy and given a large part of the County of Waterford, including the lordship of Curraghmore. Later, James I rewarded the De La Poer family with the Earldom of Tyrone.

The title Earl of Tyrone became extinct, however, for lack of a male heir, but Catherine, the surviving daughter of the last Earl, proved herself strong-willed and capable. She prevailed upon the Irish House of Lords to grant her in fee the Barony of La Poer. She married in 1717 Sir Marcus Beresford and three years later he was advanced to the Peerage of Ireland as Baron Beresford, of Beresford County, Cavan, and Viscount Tyrone. Then, in 1746, he was created the first of a new earldom of Tyrone. Catherine also gave her numerous children her own name as well as her husband's with the result that the family name is De La Poer Beresford. Her ability and aggressiveness were richly rewarded in 1789, after her death, when her son, George De la Poer Beresford, became the first Marquess of Waterford in the Peerage of Ireland. In the same year he was also created Baron of Great Britain.

The Beresford side of the family does not go back so far in the Peerage as does the De La Poer line. The first Beresford mentioned in Burke's *Peerage* is John, Lord of Beresford and Enson, County Stafford. His son Thomas fought at Agincourt in 1415. Sir Marcus who married Catherine De La Poer and was created the first to the new Earldom of Tyrone, was a direct descendant of Lord John. Incidentally, a William Burford, also called William de Bereford, was living in 1390 at Allgate, an estate formerly owned by Alice Perrers, who was at one time a mistress of King Edward III (1312-1377).[53]

Lord George, the first Marquess of Waterford, was succeeded in 1826 by his son Henry. It is said that Lord Henry "gave the clearest possible demonstration that, for all their Anglo-Norman blood, the Beresfords had assimilated the characteristics of the Irish race." Known as the "Mad Marquess" and as the "Wild Lord Waterford," his many strange exploits "were the subject of a thousand stories." Certainly, Lord Henry's grandson, Delaval, was a worthy descendant.

The third Marquess, Lord Henry, died in 1859 without heir and the titles and estates passed to his brother John (1814-1866). As a younger son, Lord John had taken Holy Orders and at the time of his brother's death was Rural Dean, Incumbent of Mullabrach, in the diocese of Armagh. He had married the beautiful and talented Christina Leslie, a descendant of John Leslie (d. 1671) who was known as the "fighting Bishop" of Raphol. John and Christina were blessed with seven children. Of these, five were sons: John (1844-1895), Charles (1846-1916), William (1847-1900), Marcus (1848-1922), and Delaval (1862-1906).[54] According to Geoffrey Bennett, the sons "combined the indomitable discipline of the Normans and the fierce but untamable spirit of the Gaels," certainly a description applicable to Lord Delaval.

Lord John who succeeded his father as the fifth Marquess, joined the Life Guards and then became a Conservative member of Parliament from County Waterford. He is described as "a great sportsman and a

Lord Delaval Beresford as a young man.

Christiana, Marchioness of Waterford, with her five sons. (Left to right) John Henry, fifth Marquess, Charles, Delaval, Marcus, William. (From a photograph taken about 1874).

Recent photo of Lady Flo's home from 1907 to 1913. It was here she died on May 19, 1913.

(Photo by Cmdr. M. G. McKinney)

Phil Young's Cafe, 217 South El Paso Street, where Lady Flo gave a party attended by John Selman.

(Photo from Aultman Collection)

popular landlord" with "a thorough mastery of the Irish land question."

Admiral Lord Charles, the second son, was the best known of the five. Entering the navy in 1859 at the age of fourteen, he rose to the command of Britain's Mediterranean Fleet (1905-07) and of the Channel Fleet (1907-09). He retired from the navy in 1911. Previously, in 1884, he served with the Nile column of Gordon's relief expedition and in 1896-97 was *aide-de-camp* to Queen Victoria. He was a personal friend of the Prince of Wales, later King Edward VII, but the two parted company because of a quarrel over a mistress. Lord Charles served in Parliament from Waterford, his ancestral home (1874-80), from Marylebone (1885-90) and from York (1898-1900). He was a recognized author and among his books were: *The Life of Nelson and His Times, The Break-Up of China, The Betrayal,* and *Memories.* He also wrote many minor articles and essays on naval and imperial questions. In 1911 he was created Baron Beresford, of Metemmeh and Curraghmore.

Lord William Leslie, the third son, joined the Ninth Lancers and served in the Afghan and Zulu wars, winning the Victoria Cross in the Battle of Ulandi. He acted as *aide-de-camp* to Edward Robert Bulwer-Lytton (first Earl of Lytton, the viceroy of India from 1881 to 1894), and later, excepting the Burmese Expedition which he accompanied in 1886, served as Military Secretary of India. With all of these accomplishments he was criticized nevertheless as "a man of remarkable natural ability [who] did not make the most of his talents." He involved himself in horse racing and became debt ridden in the amount of $200,000.00. Fortunately, he married the daughter of Commodore Cicero Price, United States Navy, and the widow of the eighth Duke of Marlborough. It was her third marriage. Her first marriage was to the elderly Louis Hammersley who, upon his death, left her an estate valued at seven million dollars. In 1888 she married the Duke of Marlborough, who died in 1892. Three years later she married Lord William Beresford. It was said that she "married once for money, once for title and once for love." At any rate, she paid Lord William's debts. His brother, Lord Charles, once remarked that "one liked him for what he was and not for what he might have been; and [after all] he did not do so badly." If any one of the five Beresford brothers is to be nominated for the accolade of ne'er-do'well, it should be Lord William. But American Puritanism gave the palm to Lord Delaval.

The fourth son, Lord Marcus, joined the Seventh Hussars and was *aide-de-camp* to the Lord Lieutenant of Ireland from 1874 to 1876. He retired from the army to devote his time and energy to the breeding and training of race horses. In 1890 the Prince of Wales appointed him to manage the Sandringham Stud, a position he held for more than thirty years.

Birth of Lord Delaval

Fourteen years after the birth of Marcus, Delaval was born. He was "understandably his mother's darling." Incidentally, the name "Delaval" came into the Beresford family when Lord Henry the Second Marquess of Waterford married Lady Susanna Carpenter, co-heiress to the Earl of Tyrconnel. One of her ancestors was George Delaval, Vice-Admiral in the fleet with which Russell scattered de Tourville's armada off Cape Barfleur in 1692.

From the American point of view, Lord Delaval was the most controversial of the five brothers and it was due almost entirely to his association with a Negress. His critics, however, tried to hide their racial prejudice by accusing him of other transgressions such as being a remittance man and a drunkard, both mortal sins, according to Puritanism. At the same time his critics praised Lady Flo. Yet the fact remains that Lord Delaval was "a hard-bitten Englishman and a shrewd *hacendado*. His better hobbies were good cattle, good grass and beautiful horses, and his weaknesses were 'Lady Flo' and hard liquor."[55]

Five sons! Five brothers! They had more in common than their Anglo-Irish blood. "All were talented men of the world, adventurers in high courage, and hard-riding sportsmen."[56] In 1922 when Marcus the last of the brothers died, it was said that "it did not seem possible that all those brothers were gone. They were so unique, both separately and together, crammed full of life and fun, and all making their mark in their own way."[57]

Today (1969), Sir John Hubert De La Poer Beresford is the Eighth Marquess of Waterford. He was born in 1933 and assumed the family titles the following year upon the death of his father. His titles include: Marquess of Waterford, Earl and Viscount of Tyrone, Baron of Beresford, County Cavan, and Baron De La Poer Curraghmore, County Waterford, in the Peerage of Ireland and a Baronet of the same in the Peerage of Great Britain, Knight of the Most Illustrious Order of St. Patrick.

The Beresford Ghost

Finally, to bring to an end this account of the Beresford family, it may be well to inform the reader of the Beresford ghost. It must be remembered that this tale is legend and not history; it may or may not have a core of historic truth. But it does give an insight into this intensely vital family.

Le Marquis de Fontenoy,[58] in a neswpaper article[59] under the caption: "THE BERESFORD GHOST STALKS THE CASTLE," wrote that the Beresford family knew of the death of Lord Delaval "before the cables flashed the news." Continuing, the author stated that

according to tradition, for two centuries the ghostly form of Lady Beresford had shown herself in the ancestral home of the family when any member has died and in this way the death of Delaval Beresford became known in the family, although, perhaps, they knew not which member of the family it was that the grim reaper had harvested. Clad in the dress of the early 18th century,[60] always with a black band of velvet around her wrist, this weird messenger made her visit this time and another descendant of the Irish earl's was known to have died.

With regard to Lady Beresford who always heralds a death in the Beresford family, there is a strange story about the black ribbon which her ghost is said to always wear on the wrist, and which figures in her portrait. It seems that she had a romantic affection for the Lord Tyrone[61] of her day, and, filled with doubts and fears as to the value of their religious opinions, they made a solemn promise to one another that whoever of the two died first should, if permitted by the Almighty, appear to the survivor for the purpose of proving the existence of the Divinity. Fifteen years later she came down one morning to breakfast looking very much agitated, with a black ribbon tied around her wrist. Her husband asked if she had hurt herself. Whereupon she earnestly entreated him not to inquire as to the cause of her wearing it, saying: "You will never see me again without it." She then eagerly and anxiously asked whether any letters had arrived, and, on being questioned by her husband, remarked that she expected to hear of Lord Tyrone's death, which she declared had taken place on the previous Tuesday. Her husband laughed. But in the afternoon a letter was brought in stating that Lord Tyrone had died on Tuesday morning in Dublin. To the amazement of Sir Tristram Beresford, his wife, instead of manifesting grief, showed a feeling of relief, and exclaimed: "I can now give you a most satisfactory piece of intelligence. I am going to become a mother. It will be a boy and an heir to your estates." The son was born within the year.

Many years afterwards, while on her deathbed, Lady Beresford revealed to her eldest son, and, to archbishop William King of Dublin her spiritual adviser and most intimate friend, the reason for her wearing the black ribbon on her wrist. She declared that on the night preceding the arrival of the announcement of the death of the last of the De La Poer earls of Tyrone, he had appeared to her sitting by the side of her bed. On her screaming with fright, he exclaimed, "Have you forgotten our promise to each other? I died on Tuesday morning at four. I have been permitted to thus appear. I assure you that the revealed religion is the true and only one by which we can be saved. I am suffering to inform you that you will seven months hence become the mother of a son, who will marry my infant heiress and that you will die in your 68th year." Lady Beresford continued, "I begged him for some convincing sign or proof, so that when the morning came I might be able to rely that his appearance had been real and not merely the phantom of my imagination. He thereupon laid his hand, which was as cold as marble, on my wrist, and where the fingers touched it the sinews shrank up and the nerves withered." "Now," said he, "let no mortal eye while you live ever see that wrist." After Lady Beresford's death, which occurred precisely as had been predicted, in her 68th year, her eldest son and the archbishop of Dublin, untied the black ribbon, and found the wrist precisely as she had described it.

It is perhaps because of this that the Beresfords are so intensely superstitious. Indeed the present head of the house, Lord Waterford,[62] on the occasion of the birth of his eldest son and heir, little Lord Tyrone, owned a magnificent house in Cavendish square, London, which unfortunately bears the number, 13. So alarmed was he lest this unlucky number cast a blighting influence over the so-called 'happy event' that he leased for a couple of months another furnished house where the child was born.

Further evidence of a Beresford ghost was given by Lou Vidal,[63] an El Paso saloonkeeper, after reading Fontenoy's story in the *El Paso Times*. Vidal served as a midshipman with Charles Beresford aboard the British man-o-war *Clio*.[64] As Vidal told the story to a *Times* reporter, it happened

one night in 1866 while we were in the Valparaiso, Chile, harbor, [when] Charley Beresford and myself were on shore leave. We started together for the town in a boat. As we neared the shore we heard a dog howl. Charley Beresford convulsively grasped my arm and in a frightened voice exclaimed, "Did you hear that? I will get bad news in my next mail from home." His face was as white as chalk and he was dispirited the balance of the evening. Nothing that we could do seemed to cheer him.

I asked him how he knew but he would not tell me, simply saying: "I was told so last night."

Sometime after this Charley came to me with a letter in his hand and tears in his eyes and he told me in a broken voice that his brother[65] had died at 9 o'clock on the night we were on shore leave, just as he had told me the following morning. Since then it always gives me a creepy sensation, myself, to hear a dog howl. I have no doubt but that the ancestral ghost of Lady Beresford appeared to him as he lay in his bunk aboard the *Clio* that night.

Several times after this during the seven years of service I saw with Charley Beresford, I saw evidence of the overpowering superstition which seemed to govern his life and acts.[66]

Lord Delaval in the Southwest

Lord Delaval James De La Poer Beresford was born on January 19, 1862. As noted above, he was the fifth of five sons and the seventh of seven children of the Fourth Marquess of Waterford. Little information is available concerning his boyhood, youth and young manhood; however, the fact is known that he served a short tour of duty as a junior officer in the Leicestershire Regiment and that he resigned his commission and came to America.[67]

At that time Great Britain was being flooded with books and pamphlets on the fortunes to be made in the cattle industry in the American West.[68] With cattle bringing forty and fifty dollars a head and the grass they ate being on public land and therefore free, the profits were "fantastic, and legendary tales of the wealth to be had in ranching spread across the nation and around the world. The result was a rush of investment from the British Isles."[69] It is very likely that this "gold fever," so to speak, combined with Lord Delaval's venturesome spirit to cause him to come to America.

Why he chose Mexico is not known. He may have been influenced, as some believe, by Edmund De Goncer, a fellow Britisher and friend, who as a plantation owner in Cuba appreciated the investment opportunities in Latin America. However, the two were never associated in the cattle business in Mexico. De Goncer was a mining man or, at least, was associated with the mining industry.[70] He may have been a drinking partner of Lord Delaval, or, if not, he was certainly addicted to drinking, for on one occasion at least, he went to Hot Springs, Arkansas for the "cure." *The Bullion,* spokesman for the mining industry in the American Southwest and northern Mexico, announced De Goncer would remain in Hot Springs "for sometime to recover from the effects of overwork."[71]

Another reason for Lord Delaval's going to Mexico may have been the cheapness of the land. The Mexican government in 1883 promulgated a colonization law which facilitated the acquisition of land by gift or purchase. The law stipulated that free grants to foreigners were not to exceed one hundred hectares[72] and that not more than 2,500 hectares could be sold to one person. But there were many exemptions. In fact, if "a little judicious bribery was employed in the right places," the amount of land one might obtain was almost limitless.[73] Further, the price of government land, as fixed by an 1878 law, varied greatly from six cents the hectare in Lower California to $2.50 in the federal district, with the average in the border states of somewhere between twelve and eighteen cents.[74] Also, it was at this time that relations between Great Britain and Mexico were partially renewed. They had been interrupted for many years in consequence of the British government's attitude during the French intervention.[75]

Delaval's Ranching Interests

Just when Lord Delaval arrived in Mexico is not known, but it was probably in 1883 when he was twenty-one years of age. Nor is it known when he purchased the Santo Domingo ranch,[76] but it was perhaps the year of his arrival. The sale is not recorded in the Registro Público de Propiedades in Juárez but the bureau clerk explained that it may have been a "verbal sale," a common practice at that time, and that Lord Beresford neglected to register it, something not unknown in the United States.

Be that as it may, it is known that Lord Delaval purchased his second ranch, Los Ojitos, on September 5, 1884.[77] It was located sixty-odd miles west of the Santo Domingo ranch with a natural corridor separating the two. As Mexican ranches go, it was small, 5,000 meters square or a few acres more than 6,000. Yet at the time of Lord Delaval's death Los Ojitos consisted of 160,000 acres and Santo Domingo of 73,500. Both were heavily stocked with fine cattle. In fact, the Beresford ranches were considered the best cattle property in all of Mexico.[78]

Los Ojitos was purchased by Lord Delaval Beresford himself, in his own name, and not by a land company, as some have claimed. To cite only two instances of such false claims, Lieutenant Britton Davis, mentioned in greater detail below, visited Los Ojitos in 1885 and wrote that the ranch was "owned by an English company whose local manager was Lord Delaval Beresford."[79] And *The Bullion* once noted that "Lord Delavel [sic] Beresford, [was] *superintendent* of the Santo Domingo ranch."[80]

Lord Delaval made periodic visits to El Paso and these were usually noted in the newspapers. One of the earliest items, dated August 28, 1884, stated that "Lord Beresford, an Englishman, residing and cowraising in Mexico, is sojourning temporarily in El Paso. He eschews the pomp and vanities of the high life to which his rank in the old country entitles [him], and partakes of the rough fare of the cowboy."[81] Another item, noting that Lord Delaval Beresford had arrived in El Paso from his Mexican ranches, stated that "marble in quantities" was recently discovered on the Santo Domingo ranch and a carload of it had been shipped to Guadalajara and that the Ojitos ranch was shipping hams and bacon to Chihuahua, . . . comparing favorably with the American product."[82] Still another item noted that "Lord D. Berresford [sic] of Chihuahua, Mexico is in the city purchasing supplies for his Sierra [Los Ojitos] ranch."[83]

A Problem with Alcohol

It was during these visits to El Paso that Lord Delaval achieved the reputation of a drunkard. No doubt remains that he drank too much, that "he was addicted to the bottle." Yet it is doubtful if he was a drunkard in the true meaning of the word. Rather, he was an alcoholic.

At least he had the characteristics of the alcoholic — compulsion and remorse. There is a story to the effect that he would go to Casas Grandes and get into fights but that he always went back when he sobered up and apologized to those whom he thought may have been hurt in some way,[84] something a drunkard would never do. Mr. McCombs, who knew him well, said that he was "a very heavy drinker but always the well bred aristocrat."[85] It is also claimed that "always he preferred dives," that "he did not seek the best society."[86] But Jack Findlay (see above, footnote 73) insists that Lord Delaval did most of his El Paso drinking in the Coney Island Saloon[87] which was the "hang-out" for cattle and mining men, as the Hotel Paso del Norte is today.

It is rather strange that little mention has been made of Lady Flo's drinking, yet she was one of Lord Delaval's drinking companions. It has been claimed that during their revelries she would boast to their friends: "We's gwine to see de Queen; she has ter see me, 'cause i'se de wife of a lord."[88] All who knew her are of a single mind, that this is not only a libel but that it pictures her completely out of character. Lady Flo may at one time have been a drunkard but she was not an illiterate blockhead. Be that as it may, about two years before his death, the couple "took the cure" and neither of them drank "very much" thereafter.[89] In fact, Lady Flo drank nothing at all during the six years following his death when she lived at 417 South Ochoa. At least her neighbors aver that she was never known to drink.[90]

Regardless of the couple's heavy drinking, their Mexican ranching interests prospered to the extent that Lord Delaval felt justified in acquiring additional property. One of his first investments was the Portales, New Mexico, ranch.[91] Another was the building at 605-609 South Oregon Street, El Paso. This property was purchased on February 1, 1901, for $2,275.00 from Paul P. Hammett. Evidently it proved a good investment because Lord Delaval's heirs retained ownership for eleven years after his death or until 1917 when they sold it to F. M. Murchison. The present owner is "Woodruff Lockhausen *et al.*"[92] The third property Lord Delaval acquired was a ranch in Canada.

The "Mexico Ranch" in Canada

As mentioned above, the great boom in Western American ranching was due largely to the free grass on the open range. By 1890, however, there was little open range left, what with the homestead acts, the coming of the railroads and the inventions of barbed wire and the windmill.[93] Cattlemen, therefore, were searching for a new frontier when word arrived of the boundless prairie of Alberta, Canada, where ranges were large enough to allow from sixty to one hundred acres to each head of cattle. In addition to the abundance of excellent food, there were water-courses, springs in plenty and a sufficiency of good shelter that kept the vast herd in fine condition with very little attention. Two men could manage 1,500 head of stock. Even in winter, "hay or grain feeding was rarely necessary, and the absence of stabling troubled the cattle only in the hardest weather."[94] Moreover, the Canadian Pacific Railway[95] was built across Alberta in 1883 and consequently Medicine Hat and Calgary[96] sprang into existence as shipping centers. The railroad was the culmination of efforts to extend control of the St. Lawrence drainage basin to the Pacific. With the completion of the road in 1885 Alberta cattlemen had access to markets in the east and west. Thus land-hungry American ranchers could hardly ignore this great bonanza to the north.

Among the first to answer the "call of the North" were the Turkey Track Ranch[97] of the Texas Panhandle and Lord Delaval Beresford. These entered Alberta in 1902.[98] They were followed the next year by "Wash" Mussett of Texas; Abner Wilson, New Mexico; Ulysses S. Grant, Texas; Steve Jones, Texas; and L. P. Pruitt, Texas.[99]

The Beresford spread was known as the Mexico Ranch and was "one of the biggest of the early lease holdings in the Western Canadian cattle country."[100] There is disagreement as to the amount of land Lord Delaval actually owned. One correspondent believes that his "original holdings were . . . about three townships and the deeded land about three sections."[101] Another states unequivocally that Beresford "never owned land in Alberta."[102] And a third notes that "land south of the [Red Deer] river was owned by the Canadian Pacific Railway but it was open range and I doubt whether Beresford did own land."[103] Previously, this same person stated that Beresford "probably leased most of his land from the Government but would have deed land for his buildings."[104]

The Mexico Ranch was located west of Steveville on the north side of the Red Deer River.[105] The ranch buildings, consisting of a house, a barn, cattle shed, chicken house, blacksmith shop and a shed for a wagon and a buckboard, were built under a high bank facing south towards the river a quarter mile away. With the exception of the house, the buildings were "chinked square log structures from driftwood timbers salvaged from the river." Their "thick walls and mud roofs [were] capable of keeping out the chill of . . . winter." The house itself "was built of hewn logs" with a roof of "split pine poles" covered with dirt.[106]

The Americans in Alberta shipped their cattle by rail from their southern ranches. Lord Delaval's first shipment consisted of 2,000 good

Texas steers and 900 saddle horses."[107] The horses were largely of the "steel dust" variety.[108] Incidentally, it is believed that Lord Delaval shipped the first burros to Canada.[109] Although he ranched on a large scale, he hired men only for round-up and shipping. The "rest of the year he depended upon the half-breed or *metis* (descendants of the French Canadian *voyageurs*) to tell him where his cattle were for round-up." He apparently fed the *metis* and supplied them with horses when their own became incapacitated.[110]

On the open range, branding was an absolute necessity. In selecting a brand some ranchers adopted numbers, others letters, or inverted letters, and still others chose monograms or some kind of composite letters in which the initials of their names formed a conspicuous feature.[111] Mexican brands were usually king size so that the *vaqueros* could read them from a considerable distance. These were called "poster" brands in Canada. The Beresford cattle brand, first adopted in Old Mexico, was U − C (U bar C), with the U on the left shoulder, the bar over the ribs and the C on the thigh. The horse brand was XT, arranged vertically with the T under the X on the left thigh.[112] In most instances Lord Delaval shipped shorthorns to Canada, but on one occasion he shipped ten train loads of Texas longhorns and turned them loose on the range. When asked why he was not branding them, he replied: "There isn't a cow within a thousand miles like these so why should I brand them?"[113]

Hansel Gordon (Happy Jack) Jackson

As Lord Delaval's cattle interests were widely scattered, from Mexico across the entire United States to Canada, he had to depend upon honest and capable foremen. This was especially true for his Alberta ranch which he was able to visit only two or three times a year. And there he was fortunate. In 1903 or 1904 Hansel Gordon Jackson, popularly known as "Happy Jack," appeared in Alberta in charge of a trainload of 1,000 Texas cattle shipped by Gordon, Ironside and Fares from the South to their Alberta range. Happy Jack had been around cattle all of his adult life. Born in Georgia, he drifted west following the Civil War and worked for several cattle outfits in Kansas, Oklahoma, the Texas Panhandle, Arizona and Old Mexico. His job of delivering the cattle accomplished, he decided to remain in Canada rather than return to the States. Consequently he accepted a job as a rider on the ranch of Lord Delaval whom he had known in Mexico. As a rider he proved himself so efficient and capable that Lord Delaval made him foreman. He spent the remainder of his life, until his death in 1942 at the age of eighty-one, on the Mexico Ranch.

There are two versions of the story as to how Happy Jack acquired possession of the buildings on the ranch. One is that Lord Delaval willed them to him. This is unlikely, however, because, insofar as is known, Beresford left only one last will and testament and that was made in 1896 (See Appendix B). The other version, which is the more likely one, has Admiral Lord Charles, the executor of his brother's estate, giving Happy Jack the buildings after first disposing of the cattle. In any case, Happy Jack staked out a homestead on the site of the buildings and by necessity became a British citizen.[114]

Lord Delaval's last visit to his Alberta ranch was made in the autumn of 1906. He ended his visit a few days before Christmas and was returning to El Paso for the holidays when he met his death in the train wreck at Enderlin, North Dakota. His body was sent to Minneapolis where it was embalmed and then it was shipped to Ireland. According to the *El Paso Herald*, Lord Delaval was interred on January 18 "in the family vault in Clonegan Graveyard, Curraghmore, in the presence of a large gathering. The Marquis *[sic]* of Waterford, head of the family, and Lord Marcus Beresford, a brother of the deceased, were the principal mourners. Admiral Lord Charles Beresford was unable to reach home from the Mediterranean in time to attend the funeral."[115]

Yet in death as he was in life, Lord Delaval is surrounded by mystery. In a letter to this writer, the present Marquess of Waterford wrote: "I still cannot find Lord Delaval's grave at Clonegon, although there is a memorial plaque in the Chapel."[116]

Lady Flo's Background

Lady Flo's name was Florida J. Wolfe.[117] The 1880 census for Salem, Marion County, Illinois, listed the "Wolf" household as consisting of the mother Nancy, 35, widowed, occupation, keeping house; son Joseph, 15, laborer; and daughter Florida, 13. The census further noted that the mother was born in Indiana, the two children in Illinois, and the father in Virginia. The 1870 census for Salem failed to show a Wolfe household, although it did list a "David Wolf, 44, male, Black, born in Virginia." He was listed as a "domestic" in the household of James S. Martin,[118] white, a man of property, born in Virginia.

The census has left a number of important questions unanswered: when and in what city or town was Florida born;[119] was David Wolf her father; were her parents divorced at the time of the 1880 census or was her father dead;[120] where was Nancy Wolf and her brood in 1870; and where did Florida go to school? According to Frank Brinkerhoff, Assistant Superintendent, Marion County Schools, the school records of Salem and Marion County "go back no further than 1891" but, he insisted, Florida "was not a graduate of Salem high school."[121] Also, it must be pointed out, two ages have been given for Florida. The 1880 census, as noted above, gave her age as thirteen and therefore her birth year would have been 1867. Her death certificate,[122] on the other hand, gave her age as forty-two at the time of death in 1913. This would have her born in 1871.

From these meager facts the only logical conclusions that can be drawn are that Florida was born in Illinois, that in 1880 she was living in Salem with her mother and brother, and that she was somewhere between nine years of age and thirteen at the time. It may be noted that those who have done research in the federal census are inclined to accept many of the statements *cum grano salis* because the "census taker" never attempted to verify the answers to his questions. And thus some persons with whom this writer talked suggested that the age on the death certificate was more likely the correct one. Yet Lady Flo implied still another age, in fact, two ages, at the time of Lord Delaval's death. Thus the contradicting statements are inconclusive.

Be that as it may, there are still a number of other unanswered questions. In fact, these form the substance of Florida Wolfe's life — these and the fact that she was compelled to live in the shadow of an Irish lord. She was ignored by the newspapers and segregated by Texas law. As examples of her segregation, when the two would come to El Paso from his ranches in Mexico, Lord Delaval would cross from Juárez alone in a cab and she would follow in another.[123] Once he was arrested and fined for appearing on the street with her.[124]

In Canada, however, conditions were more pleasant. At least there was no segregation and this may have been a factor at one time in saving Lord Delaval's life. Once on a train she protected him from an assailant and received a knife wound in her back.[125] Also, she sometimes went to the Brooks railway station, the closest rail point to the Beresford ranch, and if he were not on the incoming train, she went on to Medicine Hat to search the saloons until she found him in order to take him home.[126] She could not have done this in Texas. Thus in El Paso Lady Flo was hidden behind a wall of prejudice; however, with the death of Lord Beresford she blossomed forth as a newsworthy subject.

Lady Flo and Delaval's Will

Within five days of the lord's death the El Paso newspapers announced that he had left a will in the First National Bank of El Paso and that it provided for "Flora Woolf," his "housekeeper," in the amount of two thousand pounds "in English money." The remainder of the estate was to go to his brothers.[127] The following day the *El Paso Herald* announced in a headline on the front page: "LADY FLO WILL CONTEST THE WILL OF DELAVAL BERESFORD." In the story which followed, Lady Flo admitted that there had been "no legal marriage." But, she insisted, the two had lived together as man and wife at the Santo Domingo Ranch near Ahumada.[128] "Then," to quote her, "we moved to Los Ojitos ranch, where we have been so long together that I do not remember the number of years."[129]

The day following this announcement the *Morning Times* carried a story that the "negro woman who had lived with Beresford on his ranches in Mexico for more than twenty years has announced that she will contest the will . . . on the grounds that she was the common law wife of the decedent, and as such is entitled to a share of his estate." She declared that "while she and Beresford were never married, he held her out to the world as his wife, and that she was known through the state of Chihuahua and in this city as Mrs. Beresford." She added that Lord Beresford had intended to marry her upon his return from Canada.[130]

Lady Flo's claim that she was known as a common law wife fits a story told to Bill McGaw by Herman Lindauer, who as a small boy visited Los Ojitos ranch with his father, Sigmund. Herman Lindauer stated:

I remember sitting there in the ranch house in the twilight with my father and Lord Beresford when this tall and stately colored woman entered and Lord Beresford introduced her with all the English royalty flourishes as 'Lady Flo Beresford,' and after the hifalutin' introduction was over she came over and sat on his lap while the conversation continued.

I don't think at that time I had ever seen a colored person and I remember not being able to keep my eyes off her in wonderment. She sat there on Lord Beresford's lap and he sort of bounced her on his knee and patted her on the fanny and talked away to my father.

Lindauer further noted that this "was not a relationship to be taken lightly, as Lord Beresford was extremely pointed in introducing her as 'Lady Flo' and he did it in a manner to allay any remarks."[131] This observation that Lord Delaval was defiant and even challenging when introducing Lady Flo was also made by others who knew the couple.[132] Yet this was entirely out of character for him. He was "a man of kindly disposition,"[133] "jovial and an inveterate prankster."[134] Lady Flo said he was "a good man."[135]

As if to emphasize the common law aspect of her relationship, Lady Flo stated that she could prove in court that she had lived with Lord Delaval for twenty-five years, that she was nineteen at the time the relationship began and he was twenty-two.[136] Interpreted, this means that the relationship began in 1881 and that she, therefore, was born in 1862 and Lord Delaval in 1859, all dates obviously incorrect. In a previous statement, Lady Flo had said that she was nineteen when she joined Lord Delaval, but she did not say what year that was.[137] Using her "census age," it could have been the year 1886, a date that may be correct.

At least it is doubtful if the two were living together before 1886, for Lieutenant Britton Davis[138] visited Beresford's Los Ojitos Ranch in 1885 and in his account of the visit made nary a mention of Lady Flo. Lieutenant Davis and his squad of soldiers were pursuing a band of Apaches who had crossed into Mexico. In accordance with a treaty between the United States and Mexico, American troops were permitted to continue their pursuit of Indians on Mexican soil unless relieved by Mexican forces.[139] Davis wrote in his interesting book that "after three days and 125 miles march we arrived at a hot spring on the edge of a cattle ranch owned by an English Company whose local manager was Lord Delaval Beresford, a brother of Lord Charles Beresford. At the ranch we met Lord Delaval and his foreman. . . . I had never met an Irishman who was a prohibitionist and Beresford proved no exception." Davis added that Beresford kindly furnished him and his men enough supplies to enable them to reach the railroad thirty miles east and return to El Paso.[140] Surely, Davis, a Texan, would have commented upon the presence of a Negress at the ranch if he had seen one.

A *Problem of Legality*

Lady Flo's insistence upon a common law relationship is rather ridiculous, especially if she had a lawyer to advise her, as one newspaper item noted.[141] All American states except Louisiana[142] recognize common law. In some states only those principles and rules of the common law which were recognized before 1607, the year Virginia was settled, are regarded as having been carried over to this country; but in most states the common law, together with certain fundamental statutes, as it existed at the time of the American War for Independence, is regarded as forming a part of the law of such states. Even so, statute law is constantly nibbling away at common law and this is what happened in Texas to rob Lady Flo of her claim. Texas has long recognized common law, but a legislative act of 1893 circumscribed a part of the common law that pertains to marriage. The statute stated:

> If any white person and negro shall knowingly intermarry with each other in this State, or having so intermarried in or out of the State shall continue to live together as man and wife within this State, they shall be confined in the penitentiary for not less than two nor more than five years.[143]

In Texas, therefore, Florida Wolfe was not the wife of Lord Beresford, for she could not do under common law what she was forbidden to do by statute law. In Canada, however, Lady Flo was known and very likely would have been recognized as a common law wife.

As for its application in Mexico, common law is peculiarly English and only England and her off-spring which inherited their systems of jurisprudence from England are blessed with it. Other European countries including Spain and her colonies have Roman law which is a far cry from common law. Thus Lady Flo could hardly establish a common law claim in Mexico. Also, Mexico recognizes no form of marriage except the state ceremony, not even that of the church. This is quite likely the reason Lady Flo changed her wifely argument based on a common law marriage to one based on a state ceremony in Juárez. No record of any such ceremony exists in the Registro Civil[144] of that city. Moreover, she never produced a marriage certificate. Evidently she was trying a bluff because she no sooner stated that she had been married in Juárez than she announced that a member of the local bar had advised her to claim wages for the "twenty-two" years she had served as Lord Beresford's housekeeper. It was pointed out immediately that all wage accounts for a period longer than two years are null under Texas law.[145] And to have sued for back wages in Mexico would have been futile, as that country still practised peonage.

Meanwhile, Orlando D. Hammond, the New York attorney of Admiral Lord Charles, arrived in El Paso and prepared to take charge of the Beresford property in Chihuahua. Mexico's President Porfirio Díaz sent a special messenger to El Paso to advise Hammond that he had the president's full consent to do so. At the time this procedure was said to be most extraordinary on the part of the Mexican government. It was explained, however, that President Díaz, "after failing to find or have shown him any evidence of a legal marriage of this woman to the English lord," had taken this step to protect the Beresfords in their right to the property.[146]

A Distinguished Brother As Executor

Admiral Lord Charles Beresford, the executor of Lord Delaval's estate, arrived in El Paso on February 7, 1907. One of the first things he did was to try to arrange a meeting with Flo. She refused to see him,[147] and he made no further effort to see her. Then, when she realized that she had no legal claim to more of the estate in Mexico and Texas than Lord Delaval's will provided, she changed her tactics (See Appendix B). According to the newspaper, she came to depend "largely on Admiral Beresford's generosity," that "by appealing to him in behalf of one who had befriended his dead brother, she would move him."[148]

Lord Charles remained adamant. The will, he said, would be strictly adhered to. He further stated that he had been prepared to give her $10,000.00 but that "now she would get the money left her only through the regular channels in the chancery court of England and it would amount to only $9,600.00." He added that Flo had about one hundred cattle bearing her own brand, the letters "W" and "E" joined together [WE], on Los Ojitos Ranch, and that she likely had a few more with her brand on the ranch at Portales, New Mexico, and on the ranch in Canada. "The cattle," Lord Charles stated, "are the only possessions that the woman has aside from a few personal effects on Los Ojitos Ranch. These will be turned over to her."[149]

With this announcement, Lord Charles and his attorney left for Mexico City to obtain permission from the foreign department to probate the will in Chihuahua. The two returned to El Paso within two weeks and then left immediately for Los Ojitos Ranch where they ordered a round-up to determine the number of Flo's cattle.[150]

There is a mystery about Lady Flo's cattle or, more likely, it is only that the true story has never been told. According to Boyd: "It was customary for neighboring ranchers to work together on round-ups. Father chuckled when he discovered that the cowboys were branding half the cattle for Flo. He was still more amused to find that Beresford did not understand the significance of that procedure. Flo admitted that he did not, and added that she had had her brand recorded."[151]

This explanation of the origin of her cattle pictures Lady Flo in a bad light, a dishonest wench, if you please, and it pictures Lord Delaval as something of an oaf. From all known facts both pictures are anything but true. Moreover, if the "cowboys were branding *half* the cattle for Flo," either they could not count or Beresford had a very small herd, a premise that is certainly false. Also, the fact that Lord Charles recognized Flo's brand strongly implies that he did not question the manner in which she acquired her cattle.

As for Admiral Lord Charles himself, so long as he remained in America he was good news copy. Wherever he went he received news coverage to the almost total eclipse of Lady Flo. When he was at Los Ojitos Ranch, for instance, a news story stated that ranch life greatly agreed with him. He was said to be a good shot and had killed "a large amount of game."[152] He returned to the States and traveled to California without stopping in El Paso.[153] Then, in March, he journeyed with his New York attorney to Medicine Hat, Canada, where he remained for several days, completing details for probating his brother's will.[154]

From Canada he traveled to New York City where he was interviewed by a reporter from the *New York Times.* The resulting story stated that Admiral Lord Beresford was in America "in connection with winding up the affairs of his brother, Delaval, who died recently in Mexico *[sic]*, leaving property valued at nearly $1,000,000.00 which was bequeathed to the Admiral and his brother, Lord Marcus." Continuing, the *Times* noted that "Lord Delaval's will had to be proved in four countries, the United States, Mexico, Canada and England." As for Lady Flo, the item stated without mentioning her name that "All Lord Charles will say regarding the troubles threatened concerning the will is that matters have been adjusted." Lord Charles sailed for England on the *Teutonic* on April 3rd.[155]

Three days later the *El Paso Herald,* under a Chihuahua date-line, noted that "Admiral Lord Beresford and other devisees under the will of the late Lord Delaval Beresford of Los Ojitos, this state, have decided to keep Los Ojitos Ranch." The item further noted that "Robert L. Moss, an experienced ranch manager from Roswell, N. M., was placed in charge."[156] This arrangement continued until June, 1910, when Los Ojitos ranch was sold for $190,000.00.[157]

The Settlement With Lady Flo

When Lord Charles stated in New York that the troubles concerning Lady Flo "have been adjusted," he was a little premature. Actually two months were to pass before a settlement was reached. On May 26th, attorney O. D. Hammond returned to El Paso and employed attorney Will H. Burges to represent the Beresford interest while Judge Leigh Clark attended the interest of Lady Flo. On the 29th when an agreement was reached, Hammond made the following announcement to the newspapers:

The sum of $10,000.00 left her in the will of Delaval Beresford was paid her in cash together with an additional $5,000.00 in consideration of which she waives all claims to a community or partnership interest in the estate and declares that she was never at any time the common law wife of the deceased; that the relations between them were as master and servant, and that the entire twenty-two years she was employed on the ranch she was never the wife, in law or in fact of Delaval Beresford.

She further waives all interest of any kind or description and in the settlement papers acknowledges full payment for her services during the twenty-two years she was on the ranch.

She admits further that the sum of $10,000.00 was paid her for and in consideration of her faithful services as an employed servant and that it was left her in the will of Delaval Beresford as an act of grace and appreciation and that she had no lawful claim whatever against the estate.

For and in consideration of the $5,000.00 additional paid her she relinquishes all claims of any nature whatever against the estate, its heirs or administrators under the will of the deceased.

The newspaper story then noted:

In addition to the money received this morning Flora Wolff [*sic*] has been given the few hundred of cattle which were hers of her own right and had been branded with her personal brand. No dispute had ever been had about the cattle at all, and very soon after the death of Delaval Beresford those cattle were rounded up with the exception of a number of cows, which had calves too young to drive and had been delivered to her on a neighboring ranch.

Hammond left that afternoon for New York. He had been in El Paso four days working on the "settlement."[158]

Why did Hammond insist upon Florida Wolfe signing such an agreement, that she "was never at any time the common law wife of the deceased; that the relations between the two were as master and servant"? Was it an effort to forestall any future court action on her part, in Canada, for instance, or even in England? Or was it an attempt on the part of a staid and puritanic lawyer to protect a client from an ugly scandal? If the latter, it does not make sense. The whole world knew of the interracial relationship because a number of European newspapers had published accounts of the affair. And from the character of the Beresfords themselves, a family without a semblance of false pride, it is likely that they were unconcerned.

Be that as it may, in spite of this public announcement, ridiculous stories continued to be published. One carried in the *Montreal Family Herald* in the winter of 1908, was to the effect that a colored woman who hailed from Mexico had gone to England to claim a share in the estate of a member of the British nobility, that she had a teen-age daughter with her and that she claimed to have been married to the nobleman in Mexico.[159]

Lady Flo's Last Years

As for Lady Flo herself, she lived out her life in the role of a widow of a lord. She placed at the curb in front of her home a concrete block with the words "LADY FLO" incised in the top[160] and she insisted that her friends and neighbors address her as Lady Flo.[161] Her home, situated on the northwest corner of South Ochoa and Third Streets, was purchased on August 10, 1907.[162] There were two lots. On the one facing Third Street was a typical South El Paso, barracks-like brick apartment house containing four rental units which gave her a fair income. On the other lot was the home where she lived quietly for six years until her death. She was friendly with her neighbors without being intimate. She was recognized in the community as being a good cook, as being rather well educated, and as being able to speak fluent Spanish.[163] Her church was the Second Baptist. At church suppers she would buy what food was left and have it distributed to the poor in the neighborhood. She was looked upon as Lady Bountiful.[164] (For her will, see Appendix C.)

Lady Flo contracted pulmonary tuberculosis and died, after a short illness, on May 19, 1913. Dr. Lawrence A. Nixon signed her death certificate.[165] In so doing he listed her marital status as "widowed," thus permiting her to carry unto the grave her belief that she had been the wife of an Irish lord. The funeral was held from her home on May 22 and interment was made at Concordia Cemetery.[166] The undertaker was McBean, Simmons and Carr.

But even in death there was confusion and misunderstanding. On the day of the funeral the *El Paso Morning Times* announced in a news item: "The Negro Masonic Lodge will conduct funeral services over the body of Flora Wolfe, 'Lady Flo,' at their temple, corner Third and Kansas Streets this afternoon at 3 o'clock."[167] But the afternoon *Herald*,[168] in an advertisement, announced:

The Negro Masonic Lodge will not conduct services over the body of Flora Wolfe (Lady Flora) as stated in the *Times*. Take due notice and govern yourself accordingly.

(signed) Wm. Coleman, W. M.
Sunset Lodge, No. 76, F. & A. M.
(signed) J. A. Wilson, W. M.
Pride of the West, No. 53, F. & A. M.

Lasting Love

There have been a number of strange and unusual love affairs but none more strange and unusual than that of Lord Delaval Beresford and Florida Wolfe. There is no doubt that the two loved each other. Under other circumstances they might legally have become man and wife; however, they were denied this relationship by the Calvinistic preachings of the American frontier.

But unlike their scorners who have long since been forgotten, they have continued to live in the legends and folklore of the American Southwest and of Western Canada. Thus, in the lonely and rugged environment of the frontier, these two lives touched for a brief second in time and in so doing gave each other immortality.

APPENDIX A
LADY FLO GIVES A PARTY
by JOHN SELMAN, JR.

A few nights later as I came up the street I met several of the City Firemen. I had almost overlooked a bet. Lady Flo was giving a blow-out for us cops and Firemen at Phil Young's Cafe.[169] A certain Englishman who owned a big cattle ranch down in Mexico had come to town on one of his twice a year trips, bringing his housekeeper who we all knew as Lady Flo. This Englishman came from an old Fitted Family back in England. He was a younger son and was the real thing and a real sport. When Lord — — came to town, he blew the lid off and Mums Extra Dry flowed like water and when he bucked the Faro games the sky was the limit. Lord — — took his fun a little different from the rest of the cowmen. He was very quiet, did not do any shooting or cause any trouble, he just went on a spending spree for a couple of weeks, and Lady Flo would go her separate way and her idea of a good time was to throw a big supper for us Policemen and Firemen. This particular night she put on a big celebration and we brought along a few friends. I had with me a big lanky cowboy from down around Ballinger, and this was all new to him. He was having the time of his life until they passed around Wine and Caviar sandwiches. When he bit into it he looked a little funny and started to spit it out. Mitch, a Fireman, said, swallow it you damn fool. It is only frog eggs that got spoiled. The cowboy was game. I could see his eyes roll, but he swallowed his cud. Well, Lady Flo gave us all a present at the end of the supper. I was given a fine gold headed cane. I did not know what a cane was for, but it made me feel very aristocratic.[170]

APPENDIX B
LAST WILL AND TESTAMENT OF
LORD DELAVAL J. BERESFORD

Extracted from the Principal Registry of the Probate Divorce and Admiralty Division of the High Court of Justice.

"The State of Texas. County of El Paso.

In the name of God, Amen. I, Delaval James Beresford of 14 Wilton Crescent, London, England, of the age of thirty-four years and being of sound *mind* and disposing mind and not acting under duress menace fraud or undue influence of any person whatever do make publish and declare this is my last will and testament in manner following that is to say.

First. I direct that my body be decently buried with proper regard to my station and condition in life and the circumstances of my estate and it is my desire that I be buried at my old home at Curraghmore, County of Waterford, Ireland.

Secondly. I direct that my Executor hereafter named as soon as he shall have sufficient funds in his hands shall pay my funeral expenses and the expenses of my last sickness and all my just debts.

Thirdly. I give and bequeath to Florida Woolf of Salem, Illinois, the sum of 2000 (Two thousand pounds) in the money of England at the time of my death and I desire the said amount to be paid out of my estate in England before the division of any part of my estate among my brothers here after mentioned.

Fourthly. I give and bequeath to each of my brothers Charles Beresford, William Beresford, Marcus Beresford all of the rest residue and remainder of my estate owned by me at the time of my death whether real or personal and wheresoever situated and particularly all of the rest residue and remainder of all personal property which I may own at the time of my death whether situated in England, the Republic of Mexico, in the United States or elsewhere to be divided equally between and among my said brothers share and share alike.

Lastly. I hereby nominate and appoint my said brother Charles Beresford of Eton Square London the EXECUTOR of this my last will and testament and I further revoke all former wills made by me. IN WITNESS whereof I have hereunto set my hand and seal this the twenty second day of January in the year of our Lord one thousand eight hundred and ninety six — DELAVAL JAMES BERESFORD (Seal).

The foregoing instrument consisting of one page besides this at the date hereof by said Delaval-Beresford signed and published as declared to be his last will and testament in the presence of us who at his request and in his and in the presence of each other each of us being above the age of twenty-one years have subscribed our names as witnesses thereto — *Millard Patterson* residing at El Paso, Texas — *Maurice McKelligon* residing at El Paso, Texas."

The tumbleweed in the lower center marks Lady Flo's grave, Northwest addition of Concordia Cemetery in El Paso.

(Photo by Cmdr. M. G. McKinney)

Edmund De Goncer, English friend of Lord Delaval.

Dr. L. A. Nixson, who signed Lady Flo's death certificate.

Apartment (left) at rear of Lady Flo's house (right) on Northeast corner of Ochoa and 3rd Sts. Lord Delaval and Lady Flo stayed in the apartment building when they visited El Paso.

(Photo taken June, 1969 by Cmdr. M. G. McKinney)

Recent photo of building at 605-609 South Oregon Street once owned by the Beresford estate.

APPENDIX C

LAST WILL AND TESTAMENT OF FLORIDA J. WOLFE

The State of Texas,
County of El Paso.

KNOW ALL MEN BY THESE PRESENTS that I, Florida J. Wolfe, a feme sole, of legal age, residing in the City and County of El Paso, Texas, being of sound and disposing mind and memory and desiring to make due and proper disposition of my estate, do make, publish and declare this my last will and testament, hereby revoking any and all other wills by me heretofore made.

1. I declare that at the date of this will I am the owner of the following described property, to wit:— Lots Nos 1 and 2 in Block No. 140 of Campbell's Addition to the City of El Paso, El Paso County, Texas, together with the houses and improvements upon the same and the household goods, furnishing and similar articles therein situated. Also Lots. Nos 9 and 10 in Block No. 245 according to the map of the new town of Casas Grandes in the Municipality of Casas Grandes, District of Galeana, State of Chihuahua, Mexico, which lots I purchased from J. J. Boyd on the 29th day of June, 1906, and are more particularly described as follows, to wit:— On the North, 66 meters, bounded by lot 8; on the East 20 meters, bounded by Diaz Avenue; on the South 66 meters, bounded by 11th St.; and on the West 20 meters, alley between, bounded by lots 11 and 12 of aforesaid Block No. 245, together with all buildings and improvements thereon situated.

2. I direct that all my just debts, including funeral expenses, be paid out of my estate by my executor herein after named. In this connection I direct that no funeral service be held over my remains, but that same be taken in charge by an undertaker and buried in Concordia Cemetery; that the funeral expenses be limited to such an amount as will give my remains a decent burial.

3. To Panchita Armendariz of El Paso, Texas, who has been kind to me, I give and bequeath the sum of $15.00.

4. To Mrs. Emma Hutchison of El Paso, Texas, I give and bequeath the sum of $5.00.

5. To Flora Catarina Davis of San Diego, Cal., my God-child, I give and bequeath my crazy-quilt and my cloak that I purchased in California.

6. Such other clothing as I may own at my death, I give to Mrs. Sam, whose husband is a Chinese laundry-man to be distributed among the poor Mexicans in such manner as to her may seem best and proper.

7. After the payment and delivery of the bequests hereinbefore provided for, I give, devise and bequeath all the remainder of my property, of whatever kind or character, real, personal and mixed, and where ever situated to Joe Wolfe, Clark Wolfe and Flora Catarina Davis, share and share alike. In this connection I state that Joe Wolfe and Clark Wolfe are my second cousins and reside in the State of Indiana; that Flora Catarina Davis is my God-child and resides in San Diego, California.

8. I nominate and appoint Manuel E. Flores of El Paso County, Texas the executor of this my last will and testament and direct that no bond be required of him as such executor. I also direct that no other action be had in the matter of my estate than the filing and probating of this will and the return of an inventory and list of claims. I further direct and request that the said Manuel E. Flores be appointed and recognized as my executor in the proper Mexican Courts in making proper disposition of my estate in the Republic of Mexico as hereinbefore described.

9. To the end that my executor may promptly pay off the bequests herein made and promptly make due division of my estate as herein provided, I hereby authorize and empower my said executor to sell and dispose of any and all of the property of my said estate on such terms as to him may seem best, execute proper conveyances, receive the proceeds and distribute the same in accordance with the terms of this will. I further direct that my estate shall be closed up as speedily as possible and that when all the property has been distributed in accordance with the terms of this will that my said executor shall file in the probate court of El Paso County, Texas a full and complete statement showing in what manner the trust herein has been executed.

In witness whereof I have hereunto set my hand in the presence of the undersigned subscribing witnesses this 19th, day of May, A. D. 1913.

SIGNED: *Florida J. Wolfe*

Signed, seal, published and declared by Florida J. Wolfe, the testatrix, as and for her last will and testament in our presence and hearing, and she also made such acknowledgement to us, who at her instance and request, and in her presence and in the presence of each other, have hereunto subscribed our names as attesting witnesses, this the 19th day of May, A. D. 1913.

SIGNED: *Katherine Harper*

SIGNED: *E. B. Elfers*

REFERENCES

1 Lord Beresford's Christian name was variously spelled in the dispatches, "Delaval," "De Laval," and "Deleval." The Marquess of Waterford in a letter to this writer dated November 8, 1968, used the "Delaval" spelling. Herein the name will be spelled "Delaval" as in Burke's *Genealogical and Heraldic History of the Peerage Baronetage and Knightage Privy Council and Order of Precedence* (London, 1959, 102nd Edition). Hereinafter this work will be cited as Burke's *Peerage.*

2 *Sheldon Progress* (Enderlin, North Dakota), December 28, 1906.

3 Lord Delaval at the time of his death owned property in the city of El Paso but no ranch in Texas.

4 *El Paso Herald,* December 24, 1906.

5 *Medicine Hat News* (Alberta), January 3, 1907.

6 *El Paso Herald,* December 29, 1906.

7 J. D. Ponder, "Gambling in El Paso," *El Paso Morning Times,* July 29, 1917; also, edited with notes by Eugene O. Porter, PASSWORD XII, No. 1 (Spring, 1967), 23. J. H. Hampson who had made a fortune building railroads in Mexico was also in the game.

8 *El Paso Morning Times,* December 24, 1906.

9 The Soo line crossed into Canada at Coutts, Canada where it joined the Canadian Pacific into Lethbridge. From there one branch went to Medicine Hat and then to Calgary. Another branch went directly to Calgary. Lord Delaval's ranch lay near Brooks which is between Medicine Hat and Calgary.

10 This photograph of the wreck was printed from the negative owned by John B. Clapp of Minneapolis, Minnesota, and published here with his permission. Stuart J. Nelson of Coon Rapids, Minnesota, obtained the picture for this writer. His grandfather was the fireman on the switch engine. Incidentally, in trials held at Lisbon, North Dakota, Yard Foreman Archer and Engineer John J. Moore and Flagman Welch of the switch engine were found not guilty of manslaughter in the second degree. *Sheldon Progress,* February 22, 1907.

11 *Ransom County Independent* (Enderlin), December 27, 1906; and *Sheldon Progress,* December 28, 1906. Kent Cable, editor of the *Enderlin Independent,* kindly sent this writer xeroxed copies of the train wreck stories from the *Sheldon Progress,* the *Ransom County Independent,* and from other North Dakota newspapers. These copies along with copies of all of the material used in this paper, including a rather large number of letters, as well as the photographs, have been placed in a file, designated as the "Beresford File." It is deposited in the archives of The University of Texas at El Paso.

12 Figures concerning the number of dead and injured vary. One account placed the number of dead at eleven and the injured at forty. Another report stated that nine were killed instantly, four died later, and thirty-seven were badly injured. The *Ransom County Independent,* December 27, 1906, stated that there were "ten dead and 37 seriously hurt." The figures given herein were taken from the *Sheldon Progress,* December 28, 1906.

13 Alfred O. Boyd as told to Eve Ball, "Lady Flo," *Frontier Times,* XXVII, No. 2 (February-March, 1963). Hereinafter cited as Boyd *et* Ball, "Lady Flo." Bill McGaw, "What Happened to Lord Beresford's Ebony-black Lady Flo Still a

Mystery," *The Southwesterner*, II, No. 12 (June, 1963). Hereinafter cited as McGaw, "What Happened to Lady Flo."

14 Colin Rickards, *Bowler Hats and Stetsons: Stories of Englishmen in the Wild West* (London, 1968). The story of Lord Beresford and Lady Flo is found in chapter 22, "The Peer."

15 The *El Paso City Directory, 1906,* lists Charles W. Christley as a teamster residing at 615 South Virginia Street.

16 Authorities do not agree on the origin of the name "Medicine Hat." Histories treat of "(a) a medicine man; (b) a hat; (c) the rapids of the Saskatchewan; (d) the Breathing Spot of the Great Spirit; but the proportion of each ingredient varies with the taste and fancy of the narrative." The city lies on the main line of the Canadian Pacific Railway, seventy miles north of the international frontier. As late as 1912 it was known as a "cow town." Its history begins with the advent of the railroad in 1883. Leo Thwaite, *Alberta: An Account of Its Wealth and Progress* (New York, 1812), 175.

17 Alberta was named after Queen Victoria's daughter, Louise Caroline Alberta, wife of the Marquess of Lorne and at the time Governor-General of Canada. "Alberta," in W. Stewart Wallace, ed., *The Encyclopedia of Canada* (Toronto, Canada, 1935, 6 vols.).

18 *El Paso Morning Times,* December 24, 1906.

19 *Ibid.*

20 Boyd *et* Ball, "Lady Flo."

21 Rickards, *Bowler Hats and Stetsons,* 187.

22 McGaw, "What Happened to Lady Flo."

23 Rickards, *Bowler Hats and Stetsons,* 187-88.

24 *El Paso Morning Times,* December 28, 1906.

25 *El Paso Herald,* December 28, 1906.

26 McGaw, "What Happened to Lady Flo."

27 Ken Liddell in *Calgary Herald* (Alberta), January 18, 1961.

28 *Ibid.,* February 3, 1960.

29 R. H. (Dick) Imes, "The Old Mexico Ranch in Alberta: 1902-1942," *The Brooks Bulletin* (Alberta, 1960). Hereinafter cited as Imes, "The Old Mexico Ranch." A xerox copy of this article was sent this writer by T. R. McCloy, Librarian, Glenbow Foundation, Calgary, Canada. No date other than 1960 was given.

30 Boyd *et* Ball, "Lady Flo."

31 *Calgary Herald,* February 15, 1961.

32 *Canadian Cattleman,* October, 1950.

33 Cited by H. S. Hunter, "Around Here," *El Paso Times,* June 11, 1936.

34 McGaw, "What Happened to Lady Flo."

35 Dee Harkey, *Mean as Hell* (Albuquerque, New Mexico, 1948), 82.

36 M. C. Donnell, 85, a retired El Paso pharmacist, remembers Lady Flo very well. They attended the same church, the Second Baptist. The height figures are his, as given in a telephone conversation on December 4, 1968.

  Mrs. Helen G. Gameros of 509 S. Ochoa was a neighbor of Lady Flo during the six years she lived at 417 South Ochoa. The quote is Mrs. Gameros'. Interview, October 15, 1968.

37 *El Paso Herald,* January 7, 1907.

38 *El Paso Morning Times,* January 11, 1907.

39 McGaw, "What Happened to Lady Flo." Joe Boone, former fire chief of El Paso, remembers her from his boyhood as "black as the ace of spades." Lawrence Stevens whose "head is filled with the history of El Paso," remembers her as "ebony-black."

40 Telephone conversation with Mrs. Curtis Morris, September 21, 1968.

41 Geoffrey Bennett, *Charlie B: A Biography of Admiral Lord Beresford of Metemmeh and Curraghmore* (London, 1968), 14.

42 Ken Liddell, in *Calgary Herald,* January 18, 1961.

43 Letter dated November 27, 1968, from G. J. Barrie, Curator, Medicine Hat Museum.

44 McGaw, "What Happened to Lady Flo."

45 *Ibid.;* Rickards, *Bowler Hats and Stetsons,* 185.

46 Boyd *et* Ball, "Lady Flo."

47 *El Paso Herald,* December 29, 1906. George Toby Anthony was Governor of Kansas from 1877 to 1879.

48 Boyd *et* Ball, "Lady Flo."

49 Rickards, *Bowler Hats and Stetsons,* 188.

50 McGaw, "What Happened to Lady Flo."

51 The material on the Beresford family was gleaned from Burke's *Peerage;* Bennett, *Charlie B* (Chapter 1); *Encyclopaedia Britannica,* 1966; *Who Was Who, 1897-1916* (London, 1919); and Arthur Lyon Cross, *A Shorter History of England and Great Britain* (New York, 1930).

52 "British" is used here as an inclusive word for the peerages of the Empire. Originally, there were three separate peerages — the English, Scotch and Irish. After the Union of England and Scotland in 1707 the new creation became the peerage of Great Britain, and after the Union of Great Britain and Ireland in 1800, the new creation became the peerage of the United Kingdom of Great Britain and Ireland. Then with the establishment of the Irish Free State in 1922, the new creation became the peerage of the United Kingdom of Great Britain and Northern Ireland.

The Marquess of Waterford is of the Irish peerage which, like that of Scotland, is slowly diminishing as existing peerages become extinct and no new Irish creations are made. As an example, Ireland should be represented by twenty-eight peers, but today the number of representative peers in the Upper House is only four.

Many members of the House of Lords hold peerages in several of these groups but they use publicly only the title that is first in point of precedence.

To understand Lord Delaval's title of "Lord," it should be noted that all sons of nobles excepting those of Barons carry the honorary title of Lord and their sisters and wives, the honorary title of Lady. This is the reason one reads of Lord so-and-so being a member of the House of Commons. In the case of Barons, sons, wives and sisters carry the honorary title of The Honorable. "Peerage," *Encyclopaedia Britannica,* (1968, ed.), XVII, pp. 522-526.

53 This information was furnished by Dr. Haldeen Braddy, Professor of English, at The University of Texas at El Paso.

54 The two daughters were Kathleen Mary, the second child, and Eileen Theresa Lucy, the fourth.

55 H. S. Hunter, "Around Here," *El Paso Times,* June 11, 1936.

56 Bennett, *Charlie B*, 19.

57 *Ibid.*, 351.

58 Le Marquis de Fontenoy was one of several pseudonyms used by Philip Frederick Cunliffe-Owen (1855-1926). English born and educated, he was the eldest son of Sir Francis Philip Cunliffe-Owen and Baroness von Reitzenstein whose father was Baron Fritz von Reitzenstein of the Prussian Royal Guard. He became a United States citizen and a contributor on foreign topics to the *New York Times*. Allen Johnson and Dumas Malone, eds., *Dictionary of American Biography* (20 vols., New York, 1928-1936), IV, 600-601.

59 The Beresford ghost story was published in the *El Paso Morning Times*, January 11, 1907.

60 Ghost stories "always have an eighteenth century landscape with 'Gothic' effects." James Reynolds, *Ghosts in Irish Houses* (New York, 1947), xi.

61 The eldest son of each Marquess of Waterford uses the title of Earl of Tyrone. It is, of course, a courtesy title only.

62 This was Lord Henry (1875-1911), the sixth Marquess. His eldest son and heir was Lord John, born in 1901. He became the seventh Marquess and the father of the present Marquess of Waterford.

63 Louis L. Vidal operated a saloon at 418 Utah Street. *El Paso City Directory*, 1907.

64 The *Clio* was a sailing ship, a 22-gunned corvette. Bennett, *Charlie B*, 30.
   Vidal was telling the truth about having served as a midshipman with Lord Charles. Admiral Lord Charles, described by Vidal as "affectionately known to every man jack in the service as 'Our Charlie,'" arrived in El Paso on February 7, 1907. In an interview with reporters he was asked if he knew Lou Vidal and he replied that he had served with him as a midshipman and he remarked that he would like to see him. The two got together the same day. *El Paso Morning Times*, February 10, 1907.
   Bennett, *Charlie B*, p. 31, tells of the visit of the *Clio* to Valparaiso.

65 Vidal is mistaken. It was Lord Charles' father who died in 1866.

66 *El Paso Morning Times*, January 12, 1907.

67 Burke's *Peerage*.

68 Louis Pelzer, *The Cattlemen's Frontier: A Record of the Trans-Mississippi Cattle Industry from Oxen train to Pooling Companies, 1850-1890* (Glendale, California, 1936), 127.

69 Odie B. Faulk, *Land of Many Frontiers: A History of the American Southwest* (New York, 1968), 241.

70 At one time De Goncer was assistant superintendent of the Consolidated Company of Chihuahua. *The Bullion* (El Paso, Texas), October 6, 1891.

71 *Ibid.*, July 22, 1890.

72 An hectare contains 2.471 acres.

73 Letter to this writer dated June 30, 1968 from Jack F. Findlay, a Scotsman, who spent more than thirty years in Mexico. Born in Ceylon in 1877, he left the University of Edinburgh after two years and came to the American West. He arrived at New Orleans on his twenty-first birthday. He is the only surviving special deputy of Pat Garrett, the killer of Billy the Kid. He is also the author of two articles published in PASSWORD. Findlay wrote that he knew Lord Delaval and on

several occasions tilted glasses with him in the Coney Island Saloon, El Paso; he noted that Lord Delaval was "a very unusual person."

74 Hubert Howe Bancroft, *History of Mexico* (San Francisco, 1890, 6 vols.), VI, 490.

75 *Ibid.*, 488.

76 The Santo Domingo ranch was nine or ten miles west of Ahumada, 86 miles from Casas Grandes and about 85 miles south of Juárez.

77 *Registro Publico de la Propiedad,* Juarez, Vol. I, No. 1. The sales registration does not give the price paid for the ranch.

78 *El Paso Morning Times,* December 28, 1906.

79 Britton Davis, *The Truth About Geronimo,* ed. with intro. by M. M. Quaife (New Haven, 1929), 189.

80 *The Bullion,* August 28, 1888. *Italics* added.

81 *The Daily Times* (El Paso), August 28, 1884. During this visit to El Paso Lord Delaval completed the purchase of Los Ojitos Ranch.

82 *The Bullion,* August 28, 1891.

83 *Ibid.,* April 14, 1891.

84 Rickards, *Bowler Hats and Stetsons,* 186.

85 Letter dated November 1, 1968 from H. E. McCombs, Registrar, South Alberta Land Registration District, Calgary, to this writer. McCombs quotes his father, a retired Canadian Pacific Railway conductor who went to Alberta Territory in 1901, that "he knew Lord Beresford well who had a Negress common-in-law wife." McCombs added that his father "is 85 years of age but in good health and with a good memory."

86 *Medicine Hat News,* January 3, 1907; also *The Lethbridge Herald,* June 13, 1910.

87 Tom Powers was the bartender in the Coney Island Saloon. At the funeral of Pat Garrett he read the only service at the grave, Ingersoll's oration. Garrett was a great admirer of Ingersoll. *El Paso Herald,* March 7, 1908.

   Contractor Charles A. Goetting razed the Coney Island in 1921.

88 *The Lethbridge Herald,* June 13, 1910.

89 *El Paso Morning Times,* December 31, 1906.

90 Interview with Mrs. Helen G. Gameros, October 15, 1968. See above, footnote 36.

91 This writer has been unable to find any record of a Portales ranch. It was in either Roosevelt County of which Portales is the county seat or in adjoining Curry County of which Clovis is the county seat. In both cases county records go back no further than 1903. Very likely, conveyance records are "lost" in the maze of Territorial papers. Undated letter from Liljian Anthony, Clerk of Court, Curry County, Clovis.

92 Conveyance records in the office of the El Paso County Clerk of Court.

93 Faulk, *Many Frontiers,* 241.

94 Thwaite, *Alberta,* 106.

95 For the story of the Canadian Pacific, see F. C. Brown, *History of the Canadian Pacific Line* (London, 1929).

96 Calgary was named after a town on the Island of Mull, the homes of Colonel MacLeod of the Royal Northwest Mounted Police. It is the "child of the railway."

Thwaite, *Alberta*, 165. It is known as "the cowboy capital of the Dominion." Oren Arnold & John P. Hale, *Hot Irons: Heraldry of the Range* (New York, 1940), 135.

[97] In a letter dated October 24, 1968, to this writer, James A. Whittenburg III, superintendent, Turkey Track Ranch, Amarillo, Texas, wrote: "It is possible that the 1902 owners may have had an operation in Canada."

[98] Confusion exists as to the exact year Lord Delaval went to Canada. Imes, "The Old Mexico Ranch," gives the date as 1902 as does Rae Gordon, "Happy Jack Jackson," *Canadian Cattleman*, March, 1943; however, the *Brooks Bulletin*, May 7, 1964, quoted from the *Calgary Herald*, October 2, 1935, gives the year 1903.

[99] *Canadian Cattlemen*, October, 1950. Letter dated October 14, 1968, to this writer from C. Boone McClure, director, the Panhandle Plains Historical Society, Canyon, Texas, stated that "there is no information available in the Texas Panhandle concerning the cattlemen who moved from this region to Canada."

[100] *The Brooks Bulletin*, (Alberta) May 7, 1964.

[101] Letter dated September 13, 1968, to this writer from J. L. Nesbitt, editor, *The Brooks Bulletin*.

[102] Letter dated November 29, 1968, to Mr. H. E. McCombs, Calgary, from C. J. Christianson, Duchess, Alberta.

[103] Letter dated December 4, 1968, from H. E. McCombs.

[104] Letter dated October 30, 1968.

[105] Letter dated November 27, 1968, from J. J. Barrie, Curator, Medicine Hat Historical Museum.

[106] Imes, "The Old Mexico Ranch."

[107] *Canadian Cattlemen*, October, 1950.

[108] "Steel Dust" horses are not so much a breed as a color which is established through breeding. It is a dark steel color with all the hairs in the coat grey, white and black and not arranged in any particular pattern. Another distinguishing mark is the dark skin; whereas "grey" horses have light skin. It is believed that they are descended from the Arabian. They have great speed, strength and stamina. Interview with Miss Gracie Samuels, El Paso horsewoman and trainer.

[109] Ken Liddell, *Calgary Herald*, February 15, 1961.

[110] Letter from H. E. McCombs, December 4, 1965.

[111] Anon., *Historical and Biographical Record of the Cattle Industry and the Cattlemen of Texas and Adjacent Territory* (St. Louis, 1895), 63-65.

[112] Letter from J. J. Barrie, November 27, 1968.

[113] Letter from H. E. McCombs, December 4, 1968.

[114] Imes, "The Old Mexico Ranch;" D. A. McCannel, "Happy Jack's Life was Story of the Early West," *Calgary Herald*, October 12, 1935, reprinted in *The Brooks Bulletin*, May 7, 1964.

[115] *El Paso Herald*, January 19, 1907.

[116] Letter dated November 8, 1968.

[117] There was no consistency in the spelling of Lady Flo's name. In the 1880 census it was spelled "Wolf;" in Lord Delaval's will, "Woolf;" in the "settlement" with the Beresford estate, "Wolff;" and in the El Paso newspapers, in her will and on her death certificate, "Wolfe." Herein her name will always be spelt "Wolfe" unless it is spelled otherwise in a quotation.

118 In a letter dated November 18, 1968, to this writer, Mrs. Harry L. (Daisy Martin) Kirkpatrick, Figurehead House, Dolliber's Cove, Marblehead, Massachusetts, wrote: "My father was James S. Martin and he came from Virginia but I was born in 1894 and my father died when I was thirteen. I never heard of the Wolfes and cannot refer you to anyone as I am the last of that branch of the Martin family."

119 The birth records for Marion County, Illinois, go back only to 1877. Letter from the County Clerk of Court, August 29, 1968. The Bureau of Statistics of the State of Illinois, Department of Public Health, did not begin to function until January 1, 1916. Undated letter from the Bureau.

120 The 1880 federal census had a column, "widowed or divorced." No distinction was made between a natural widow and a divorcee.

121 Letter dated November 20, 1968, from Mr. Brinkerhoff to this writer. He also wrote that "Salem is now a lily white community; the last native born colored lady died last year." She may have been the last source of information about the Wolfe family. By the way, Mr. Brinkerhoff gave my request for information about the Wolfe family "publicity in the paper and over the local radio station, but no success."

122 Death Certificate Registered No. 185, Office of the Clerk of Court, El Paso County, Texas.

123 Told this writer by Joe Boone who, as a boy, remembers the "Beresfords."

124 *El Paso Morning Times*, December 31, 1906.

125 Letter dated November 1, 1968, from H. E. McCombs. (See footnote 85).

126 Letter dated December 4, 1968, to this writer from H. E. McCombs, again quoting his father.

127 *El Paso Morning Times*, December 28, 1906. Admiral Lord Charles cabled Judge Clark, the legal representative of the deceased, to have the remains shipped to Minneapolis and to open the will. *Medicine Hat News*, January 3, 1907.

128 Ahumada is about 85 miles south of Juárez on the road to Chihuahua City.

129 *El Paso Herald*, December 29, 1906.

130 *El Paso Morning Times*, December 30, 1906.

131 McGaw, "What Happened to Lady Flo."

132 Mrs. Florence Cathcart Melby of El Paso told this writer that Lord Delaval's defiance when introducing Lady Flo was a matter of common gossip among the American ranchers in Mexico.

133 *El Paso Herald*, December 24, 1906.

134 Ken Liddal in *Calgary Herald*, February 3, 1960.

135 *El Paso Herald*, December 29, 1906.

136 *Ibid.*, January 7, 1907.

137 *El Paso Morning Times*, December 30, 1906.

138 Lieutenant Britton Davis was the son of Edmund J. Davis, the last Reconstruction Governor of Texas, and the brother of Judge Waters Davis (1862-1935), prominent El Paso attorney. At one time Judge Davis was associated in law practice with W. H. Fryer and Dan Jackson. He named his son Britton after the lieutenant's uncle. *El Paso Times*, April 15, 1935.

139 The treaty by which United States and Mexican troops could mutually continue their pursuit of Indians across the boundary was made in 1882. H. H. Bancroft, *History of Arizona and New Mexico: 1530-1888* (San Francisco, 1890), 571.

140 Davis, *The Truth About Geronimo*, 189-191.

141 *El Paso Morning Times*, February 10, 1907.

142 The state of Louisiana has the Napoleonic code.

143 *Vernon's Annotated Civil Statutes*, Art. 492, p. 4607.

144 This writer searched the marriage records at the *Registro Civil*, Juárez, for the years 1881 to 1906 without finding any reference to Delaval Beresford and Florida or Flora Wolfe, Woolf, Wolf, and Wolfe. Humberto Benítez M., a clerk in the *Registro Civil* signed a statement to this effect.

145 *El Paso Morning Times*, February 10, 1907.

146 *El Paso Herald*, January 12, 1907.

147 *Ibid.*, February 13, 1907.

148 *Ibid.*

149 *Ibid.*

150 *Ibid.*, February 25, 1907.

151 Boyd *et* Ball, "Lady Flo."

152 *El Paso Herald*, March 6, 1907.

153 *Ibid.*, March 7, 1907.

154 *Ibid.*, March 30, 1907, quoted from *New York Times*, same date.

155 *Medicine Hat News*, March 21, 1907.

156 *El Paso Herald*, April 6, 1907.

157 *The Lethbridge* (Alberta, Canada) *Herald*, June 13, 1910.

158 *Ibid.*, May 29, 1907.

159 Quoted by Imes, "The Old Mexico Ranch."

160 Every El Pasoan who remembers Lady Flo remembers the concrete block but no one knows when it was removed, by whom or where it is now. If found, it would make a good marker for Lady Flo's grave.

161 Told this writer by Mrs. Helen Gameros as well as by others.

162 The house was on the northeast corner of the intersection of Third and South Ochoa Street, Block 140, Lots 1 and 2, Campbell Addition. Lady Flo purchased it from Laura Pettibone, a widow, "in consideration of the sum of Five Thousand and no/100 Dollars." El Paso County Clerk's Office, Deed Book 94, p. 381. Upon Lady Flo's death the house was sold to Nick and John Koukiakis who operated the De Luxe Cafe across the street from the State National Bank. Today Robert M. and Alicia O. Martinez own the property, having purchased it in 1967.

163 Told this writer by Mrs. Elisa Domínguez de Lelal whose father worked for Lord Delaval on his Ahumada ranch, She claims that her father was the lord's closest friend.

164 Told this writer by Mr. M. C. Donnell. (See footnote 36.)

165 Death Certificate Registered No. 185, El Paso County Clerk's Office.

166 Lady Flo was buried in the Northwest Addition, Tier 9, Grave 15, Section3. The burial records for Concordia Cemetery are kept by Bob Narzinsky and may be examined at the Pioneer Monument Company, 3803 Alameda Avenue.

167 *El Paso Morning Times,* May 22, 1913.

168 *El Paso Herald,* May 22, 1913.

169 Phil Young's Cafe was also known as "The Cafe Saloon." It was located at 217 El Paso Street and was one of the three most popular drinking places in El Paso, the others being the Coney Island and the Wigwam. *El Paso City Directory, 1896-97.*

170 From an unpublished manuscript entitled John Selman of El Paso by John Selman, Jr. Leon Metz, Archivist at The University of Texas at El Paso, is editing the manuscript for publication. Metz is the author of *John Selman-Texas Gunfighter,* published by Hastings House. It seems rather strange that Selman did not mention the fact that Lady Flo was a Negress although elsewhere in the manuscript he used the word Negro. It is also strange that he did not mention Lord Beresford by name. It is impossible to establish from the manuscript the date of the party.

ACKNOWLEDGEMENTS

In researching this study I discovered that my material was scattered to the four corners — Mexico, Texas, New Mexico, Canada, Ireland and England. Since travel to these far places was out of the question, I had to depend upon others for much of my material. I wish to take this opportunity, therefore, to thank those who graciously helped me in my quest for information: Lord John Hubert De La Poer Beresford, the Marquess of Waterford, and his brother, Lord Patrick Beresford; Mr. Kent Cable, editor, *The Enderlin* (North Dakota) *Independent;* Mr. T. R. McCloy, Librarian, The Glenbow Foundation, Calgary, Canada; Mr. J. L. Nesbitt, editor, *The Brooks Bulletin* (Alberta, Canada); Mr. H. E. McCombs, Registrar, South Alberta Land Registration District, Calgary, Canada; J. J. Barrie, Curator, Medicine Hat (Alberta, Canada) Historical Museum; Mr. Stuart J. Nelson, Coon Rapids, Minnesota; Mr. John B. Clapp, Minneapolis, Minnesota; Mrs. Colleen Majors, Assistant Librarian, State Historical Society of North Dakota; Mr. Frank Brinkerhoff, Assistant Superintendent of Schools, Salem, Illinois; and Señor Juan Holguín L., Chihuahua, Mexico, President, Chihuahua State Historical Society.

I also wish to thank all of those El Pasoans who helped me with their special knowledge or otherwise aided me in making the study more complete: Mr. Tony Chávez, Clerk of Probate Court, El Paso County; Mr. Jack F. Findlay, Dr. John M. Sharp, Professor of Modern Languages, The University of Texas at El Paso; Mr. Jack T. Niland, El Paso attorney; Mmes. Virginia Hoke and Emma Evans of the Lea-Hertzog Room, El Paso Public Library; Miss Gracie Samuels and Miss Ronni Rosenfeld who helped with the research and typed the manuscript.

Finally, I wish to express my deep appreciation to Jesús Martínez, Jr., a student at The University of Texas at El Paso and a member of the El Paso Police Department, for helping me research the archives in Juárez and also for finding older Spanish-speaking residents of El Paso whom we interviewed.

— EUGENE O. PORTER

El Paso, Texas
October 1, 1969

Curraghmore, the Beresford family home, Waterford, England.

Rear-Admiral Lord Charles Beresford in 1903. Lord Charles was in El Paso on February 7, 1907 as executor of Lord Delaval's estate.

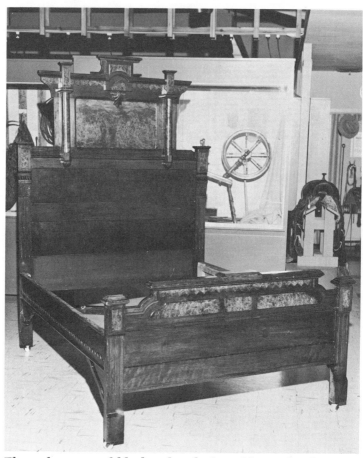

The mahogany and black walnut bed used by Lady Flo and Lord Beresford at their ranch in Canada.

Photo courtesy J. J. Barrie, curator,
Medicine Hat (Canada) Historical and Museum Foundation.